OLD WORCESTER CHINA

John Bedford

WALKER AND COMPANY
NEW YORK

*Vase and cover, painted in
the style of the* famille verte
*by 'the fine-brush painter'.
c. 1750–5. Lund's Bristol
or early Worcester. 13¾ in.
high.* (Victoria & Albert
Museum.)

Printed in Great Britain

Contents

INTRODUCTION   4

1.   BEGINNINGS AT BRISTOL   5

2.   DR WALL OF WORCESTER   10

3.   BLUE AND WHITE   18

4.   TRANSFER PRINTING   21

5.   WORCESTER 'JAPANS'   29

6.   COLOURED GROUNDS   34

7.   WORCESTER BIRDS   38

8.   FLOWERS AND FRUIT   41

9.   ARMORIAL WARES   46

10. MOULDING AND MODELLING   48

11. THE FLIGHTS, THE BARRS AND
         THE CHAMBERLAINS   54

12. MARKS   63

Introduction

In the early 1750's a group of Worcester professional and business men decided to begin making 'china or porcelain ware'. It could never have occurred to them that not only would their enterprise endure for two centuries—as it has so far done—but that the wares they were making in the ordinary way of trading would become the much-desired quarry of collectors for generations ahead.

'Old Worcester' at its best has attractions which few lovers of china can resist—and it is in a spirit of affection that one prefers this old-fashioned word to 'porcelain'. It is true that many of the shapes, decorative styles and motifs used at the factory were borrowed from the Continent or the Far East, often even at second hand through other English establishments like Chelsea and Bow. But in aiming itself at the growing middle-class public of its day, and in very accurately assessing that public's taste, Worcester's productions, wherever inspired, generally took on a characteristic and unmistakable English flavour.

The range of Worcester's achievement has been astonishing. So too, is the extraordinarily high standard of workmanship which it has maintained throughout all its history: many a collector is content to identify a piece only by the qualities shown in its potting.

This little book is added to the 'Collectors' Pieces' series in the hope that it will introduce to a wider public a field of collecting which still offers a niche or two to those of modest means. I would like to express my gratitude for help and advice given by Mr Cyril Shingler, Curator of the Perrins Museum at Worcester, Mr David Mitchell of Sotheby's, and to the staff of the Victoria & Albert Museum, London.

1. Beginnings at Bristol

In the beginning, Worcester was Bristol. About the year 1748, in an old glasshouse on the banks of the River Avon, a copper merchant and brassfounder named Benjamin Lund started to make porcelain like that produced at Bow and Chelsea during the previous three years. Five years later, Lund sold out to a partnership of business men and other prominent local citizens at Worcester. They wanted to bring trade to their town and they saw its special advantages for the potting business—cheap transport for materials up the River Severn, easy access to fuel supplies, plentiful labour, and a prosperous countryside with money to spend. The little Bristol factory, together with the tools of the trade—and also, it seems, some of the workmen—were gradually transferred to Severnside; and thus began the two-hundred-year-old story of a famous enterprise which entertained Georgian kings and queens, and which still opens its doors to visitors interested in seeing how fine china is made.

HARD-PASTE AND SOFT-PASTE

The porcelain made by Lund and his successors at Worcester was not of the same type which Court and Town had been buying for a century or more from China and for the last twenty years from continental sources like Meissen, near Dresden. This so-called 'real' porcelain was made from two forms of feldspathic rock—popularly China stone and China clay—fused together at immensely high temperatures. The secret of this formula and the technique of reaching these high temperatures had been known for centuries to the Chinese, but it had only recently been rediscovered at Meissen, and was still unknown to potters in England and France. So the product of potters in these

Four-footed teapot, Lund's Bristol or early Worcester. c. *1752–5.* (Ceylon Tea Centre.)

countries was usually a substitute for the real thing, using broken-up glass, the ashes of bones, clay and other materials which could be fired at lower temperatures.

This 'soft-paste' porcelain lacked the cold, brilliant perfection of the 'hard-paste' made by Chinese and Saxon potters; but it had qualities of its own which have long endeared it to connoisseurs.

The main reason for the difference lies in the nature of the materials used. In hard-paste porcelain, body and glaze are closely related to each other—they are really the same substances in different stages of decay, so that when fired together they unite completely. For this reason they are impervious to liquid, and even to normal scratching. When a piece is broken it shows a glassy fracture, 'moist and lucid', as one English maker described it. Soft-paste porcelain on the other hand, like earthenware, is first fired in the 'biscuit' or unglazed state, and after decoration it is given a coating of lead-glaze and fired in a 'glost' kiln at a lower temperature. This means that soft-paste is not nearly so resistant to liquid or stains as is hard-paste. Pieces can easily be scratched with an ordinary nail-file or knife, and they show a grained or sugary surface; 'when they are broke', said the same manufacturer, 'they seem as dry as a Tobacco Pipe'.

6

But it is this fact of firing on the lead glaze afterwards, and the way it 'sits' on the surface rather than becomes absorbed into it, which gives soft-paste one of its greatest charms—a unique depth and richness in the decoration, which seems to glow through the glaze as though illuminated from below. The body itself is softer, and consequently more sympathetic to the touch—the French expression *pâte tendre* (literally 'tender paste') is very apt. It is true that the forms of pieces made in soft-paste can be irregular or warped, often wildly so; but just as a house made from old materials acquires an interesting texture by very virtue of its irregularities, so these pleasant variations from academic perfection only serve to whet the appetite of the true *aficionado*.

UNIQUE WORCESTER FEATURES

Having said that, one must now differentiate between the products of Worcester and those of Chelsea and Bow. After the first halting efforts, Worcester soft-paste showed 'defects' far less than did the other English factories. At Chelsea, the potters had added materials like chalk and lime to their glassy 'frit' of crushed pieces of old glass and pottery. At Bow, greater stability had been provided by using the white ashes of animal bones—as in the German *Milchglas*, which these porcelains greatly resembled. At Bristol, however, a very substantial proportion of the 'mix' consisted of soapstone, a steatized granite. At the very beginning of activities there, Benjamin Lund had taken out a licence to mine this product in Cornwall, and it was used at Worcester all through the eighteenth century, until it was eventually superseded by various versions of the standard English bone china.

The use of this soapstone gave the Worcester wares much greater stability, and therefore more regular forms and greater durability. The factory was able to make proud claims on these lines—or have other people make them on its behalf. 'A manufactory at Worcester' announced the

Handmaid to the Arts in 1758, 'hath lately produced, even at very cheap prices, pieces that not only work very light, but which have great tenacity, and bear hot water without more hazard than the true China ware.'

Early Worcester porcelain is sometimes so hard as almost to have the feel of hard-paste itself, being finer grained, and therefore less 'sugary' than most soft-pastes. The lead glaze is also more hard and even than most soft-pastes. 'It fits well,' as one appreciative critic has said. It resists scratching and is very rarely crazed, i.e. has its surface broken by fine lines, an effect caused by uneven contracting of glaze and body during firing. This is one of the reasons why Old Worcester usually retains its brilliance better than most soft-pastes: such cracks inevitably accumulate dirt and dis-coloration over the years.

Another distinctive feature is that whereas on other wares, especially those of Chelsea, the glaze can form in 'drops'

Moulded dish or tureen stand, with chinoiserie *decoration and also painted in underglaze blue. The 'TF' or 'maimed* yu' *mark in underglaze blue.* c. *1755.* (British Museum.)

(Top row)

Dish with claret ground border painted with flowers by the 'cut-fruit' painter.

Cup and saucer with 'hop-trellis' pattern and turquoise ('sky-blue') border.

Jug with armorial bearings (Colles of Kilkenny) and landscape painted in colours.

(Middle row)

Two-handled vase painted with flowers by James Donaldson.

Mug with scale-blue ground and 'criss-cross' flowers.

Moulded leaf-dish with Meissen flowers.

Potiche-shaped vase with 'dry-blue' flower painting.

Vase with painting of horses by Jeffrey Hamet O'Neale.

(Bottom row)

Bowl with yellow ground and a reserved panel having transfer-printing coloured over.

Sugar box, with 'apple-green' ground and bird painting in reserved panels.

Coffee-pot, with the 'partridge' pattern in Kakiemon colours.

'Scratch-cross' sauce-boat, painted in colours.

Dish from the 'Lord Henry Thynne' service with blue and gilt border, painted with a landscape.

Potiche with pink ('peacock') scale ground and flower painting.

All from the Perrins Museum Collection, by courtesy of the Worcester Royal Porcelain Co. Ltd.

around the footrims, with Worcester one of the useful (though not invariable) means of identification is the fact that the glaze is absent from the edges—for example, of footrims. This occurs not as a result of shrinkage, as is often stated: the surplus glaze was usually cleaned away, or, as appears to have been done in certain instances when the glaze was applied by brush, stopped short of the rim. This practice, Mr Shingler tells me, is still followed at the factory. It is worth noting also that if you lift a piece to the light, you may see a greyish or bluish tone to the glaze, due to a touch of cobalt which has been added to counteract the 'yellow' hue of which the eighteenth-century buyer—in his admiration for Chinese hard-paste—so greatly disapproved. Sometimes there is a distinctly greenish tone: this will be due to the 'blueing' just mentioned or to the presence of iron as an impurity.

Worcester's high standards in the way of materials were also observed in the potting methods. Shapes and styles, though not particularly original, were well proportioned and for the most part free from the extravagances often found at Chelsea or on the Continent. The workmanship is highly efficient; such close attention is given to small details that management skills at the factory, like those at Wedgwood's later in the century, must have been of a very high order. In fact, after a few initial difficulties, the wares produced during the whole of the First Period, as it is called, show a 'professional' character which is often more useful than any other consideration in identifying a piece.

Such qualities as these were obviously likely to recommend themselves to the economically minded buyer of china, and it now seems clear that, from the beginning, the company of business men and professional men who directed the fortunes of the factory in the early days were shrewdly setting their sights at the wider public beyond the Court and the nobility—the country gentry, the increasingly prosperous professional and business classes—who wanted to buy fine and yet practicable wares at reasonable prices.

9

2. Dr Wall of Worcester

The Bow factory had called itself 'New Canton', and the young establishment on Severnside also showed its deep respect for Far Eastern porcelain by advertising itself as the 'Worcester Tonquin Factory'. There were fifteen original subscribers to the company, the best known of them being Dr John Wall and the manager William Davis. The first-mentioned, who has given his name to the whole of the period of manufacturing down to 1783, was a practising doctor, the author of medical treatises and a competent amateur painter, some of whose work, it is claimed, is to be seen on the company's porcelain. For premises they took over an old mansion on the riverside called Warmstrey House, which had a convenient 'slip' or inlet, where vessels could discharge cargoes of the necessary raw materials and fuel.

The engraving shown on the next page was published in the *Gentleman's Magazine* in 1752.

BRISTOL/WORCESTER

It is evident that for the first few years there was an overlap in activity between Bristol and Worcester. The same moulds appear to have been used at both places, and at this date it is often difficult to decide whether particular specimens were made in one place or the other. Those made at Bristol, when they can be certainly identified, are now usually known as Lund's Bristol, in preference to the former term Lowdin's or Lowris' Bristol, after the name of the old glasshouse. The term also offers a useful distinction between these wares and those made in the hard-paste porcelain made at Bristol some twenty years later, which is known as Cookworthy's or Champion's Bristol. The first name stands for the Plymouth Quaker chemist who re-

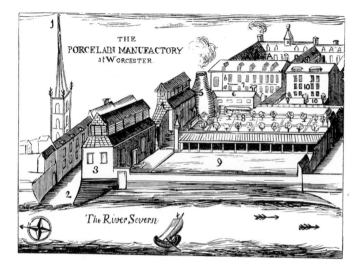

THE WORCESTER FACTORY AT WARMSTREY HOUSE IN THE
YEAR 1752.

'*1. St. Andrew's Church. 2. Warmstrey slip, where the vessels
landed their clay. 3. Biscuit kilns. 4. Glazing kilns. 5. Great kiln
for segurs (saggars?). 6. Pressing and modelling gallery. 7. Rooms
for throwing, turning and stove drying the ware on the first floor,
a, of the chamber floors. 8. The garden. 9. The yard for coals.
10. Mr Evett's house and garden, landlord of the premises.*'

discovered—independently of both China and the Continent—the secret of hard-paste porcelain; and the second
for the manufacturer already quoted (see page 6), one
Richard Champion, who worked the formula at Bristol
between 1770 and 1781.

Some Lund's Bristol puts its place of origin beyond doubt
by having the name of the town (sometimes spelt 'Bristoll')
impressed or embossed in countersunk relief in the body.
These pieces include figures of 'Chinamen', perhaps copied
from originals in the famous snowy *blanc-de-chine* hard-paste

porcelain of Te Hua: they may bear, in addition, the date 1750, which also gives them a pre-Worcester origin. The 'Bristol' mark also appears on some sauce-boats and butter-boats moulded in relief after a silver shape (page 15), and these are accompanied by a whole series with close family resemblances which could have been made equally at Bristol or Worcester. Among them are the charming double-handled sauce-boats shown here (page 21).

Collectors find enormous pleasure in trying to allot these early wares to one place or the other; but in so short an account as this, one must be content to treat all these wares, whether marked or not, as 'Bristol/Worcester'.

When the wares are painted in enamel colours the paste of this era has a warm ivory tone; but those in underglaze blue show a bluish or greyish cast. This effect is thought to have been due to the cobalt pigment having 'flown' in the kiln; the blue painting is certainly often very blurred. The colour work, however, is usually most delicately done, and is among the most charming of any Worcester ware.

EARLY CHINOISERIE

Among these very earliest wares we find the first of the famous *chinoiserie* used at Worcester.

It has already been suggested that the English potters

Teapot, early Worcester, painted in colours with the 'Spinning Maiden' pattern. (Sotheby & Co.)

thought of themselves as being in direct competition with the Far Eastern porcelain which was at that time coming into Europe in vast quantities in the holds of the East Indiamen. Not only did the West follow Far Eastern pottery in its forms, and as far as they could the appearance of the bodies used, but they also adopted similar decorative themes. Sometimes these were literal copies, often quite successful, sometimes the merest travesties.

As time went on, however, potters in the various European countries developed their own versions of the Chinese and Japanese themes, some of which almost rank as original creations. In the English potteries especially, this adaptation of Far Eastern ideas, seen through the eyes of a native craftsman who had no idea of the real significance of the original themes—and often picking up a touch of rococo frivolity on the way—provided a host of enchanting designs. They bodied forth a kind of dream world where willow trees grew apples, and where tall Chinese ladies and gentlemen wandered through blossoming gardens and across bridges in romantic landscapes, surrounded by such brightly coloured exotic birds and animals as were never seen by land or sea.

When Worcester came into being these *chinoiserie* were in full spate at the existing factories. They had been first developed at Meissen early in the century, and were then strenuously taken up at Sèvres, Chantilly and other French porcelain and faience factories. They had also been seized upon by our own Chelsea and Bow: and it was usually through one or other of these intermediaries that Worcester found its inspiration.

This is not to say that all the work at Worcester was imitative. Later in the century the work there did tend to become rather standardized; but in these early days there is a great deal which stands up in its own right as a real contribution to ceramic decoration.

Among the early overglaze enamel painting in the colours mentioned above, there are some wares decorated by one

(Above) *Milk jug painted in colours and gilt.* c. *1760–5. 3½ in. high.* (British Museum.) (Below) *Vase and mug painted in the styles used on Bristol white opaque glass.* c. *1750. 4⅝ and 3¼ in. high.* (Victoria & Albert Museum.)

artist in particular whose name is unknown to us but who is generally called 'the fine-brush painter'—we shall often in Worcester's history be coming across this method of identifying unknown artists' work. With great delicacy of line he drew Chinese and European figures, birds and flowers, in the very pleasant palette seen on our colour plate.

Much of the work on these early wares uses the colours of the *famille verte*, one of the great families of Chinese porcelain in which green is an outstanding colour: the subjects show birds and figures set among plants, rocks and flowers. Another style is shown in the 'Spinning Maiden' pattern which appears on our teapot (page 12), where a design 'printed' in outline of brown or black is coloured over with enamels in bright red, blue, green and pink. There are also Chinese landscapes in crimson monochrome on a pale yellow ground.

Quite a different type of decoration has the figures 'pencilled' in black. It is seen on the plate on page 17 with the familiar subject of a boy seated on an ox. This technique, often in panels on a yellow ground, is sometimes mistaken for transfer printing (see page 21), since the same subjects are often found in both. It was, however, taken directly from a Chinese practice in use at the imperial factories in the early eighteenth century.

There were, of course, many instances of this kind of exchange between East

14

and West—which did not always stop at the one-way process. In the Worcester Works Museum, for example, there is a saucer which is 'pencilled' in black with a European subject copied from a Chinese copy of a European engraving.

Another recognizable hand seen on the Bristol/Worcester wares is of a man who liked to draw tall Chinese figures with long, talon-like fingers, also birds with long curled tails: it is seen on the mug (*opposite*).

A more literal following of a Chinese manner is seen in the 'mandarin' styles also used on the early wares. They are shown in our milk jug (*opposite*); the bodies are often obliquely fluted and moulded in the lower part with palm sprays.

Chinoiserie also appears on some of the moulded dishes or tureen stands which appear in the Bristol/Worcester days. Our specimen (page 8) is moulded in high relief with lizards, birds, fishes, insects and flowers among rococo scrolls. It bears in under-glaze blue the mark which was once thought to be the monograph TF, for Thomas Frye of Bow, at a time when a whole class of these early moulded wares (page 48) were attributed to that factory. They included many dishes, teapots, tureens, and sauce-boats etc. with rich mouldings in the styles of contemporary silverware and painted with dainty vignettes of *chinoiserie* and flowers. After analysis of a dated tureen owned by Mr Dyson Perrins, the mould for which was still at Worcester—this generous collector actually consented to have a piece broken off for the purpose—it was found that they had the requisite proportion of soapstone and must therefore be ascribed to Worcester. The mark is now referred to as the 'maimed *yu*', on Mr Hobson's suggestion that it might be a broken version of the Chinese character for jade which is often found on porcelain. There are later examples of these large dishes where the same mould has been used, but the decoration is from coloured enamels or even by transfer printing: one such, in the Schreiber collection at the Victoria & Albert

Museum, has the odd conjunction of an eighteenth-century ship which is flying the British flag and sailing between two of Robert Hancock's classical ruins.

THE 'SCRATCH-CROSS' FAMILY

This name is given to a class of 'Bristol/Worcester' wares which have an incised cross or a couple of short strokes on the base or even just a nick on the inside of the footrim. Some of them also have marks painted in blue or other colours. Collectors have long speculated about the purpose and significance of these marks.

The wares fall into a recognizable group also by reason of their forms. There are two types of mug, one of which is a slightly waisted cylinder; the other, rather taller, is of an ogee shape. There is a pear-shaped jug with a scroll handle, and a sauce-boat in the form of moulded leaves, boldly painted with contemporary figures or *chinoiserie* in underglaze blue or overglaze enamels—the form seems to have a Meissen origin. A coffee-pot in the series has tasteful painting of foliage, and a ewer and basin are painted in shades of brown with an amusing picture of a bird perched on a tree-stump and a snail on the ground below, both apparently trying to stare each other out. Pieces like this are often said to have noticeable fissures where handle meets body, suggesting difficulties in the kiln.

This fact may well support the theory which has been advanced that the marks—which appear on the products of other factories as well—were used to indicate experiments with different pastes; and it has been shown by analysing one specimen that some of them contain rather less magnesia than was usual at Worcester. Mr Bernard Watney has pointed out that the alchemist's sign for talc or soapstone was a saltire cross; and it is known that there was a chemist among the proprietors at Worcester. On the other hand, Mr Dyson Perrins, whose magnificent collection is to be seen at the Worcester Works Museum today, came to the conclusion, after discussing the matter with workmen there, that they were simply batch marks, as in other factories, indicating the stint carried out by a particular man. Mr Frank Tilley, concurring, thought that the variations might represent different tally marks for a dozen, a gross or some other number.

As to the Bristol/Worcester question, there are plenty of links with both places. The incised stroke marks appear together with the impressed 'Bristoll', while typical jugs and mugs have decoration and even dates which insist upon an undoubted Worcester origin.

Moulded leaf-dish with 'primitive' transfer printing. c. 1756–7. Plate pencilled in black. c. 1755. (Victoria & Albert Museum.)

3. Blue and White

English blue and white porcelain has for a long while now been a collecting field in its own right. It has fervent admirers whose collections are worth a good deal more today than they were only a few years ago, when these wares were greatly undervalued. Even today, this class of English porcelain stands as one of the most accessible fields for the connoisseur of modest means.

Unlike so many things bought for decoration or delight, 'blue and white' loves its own company. You can without monotony fill a cabinet or a whole niche of shelves with it, varying it only in the matter of shapes and styles.

Of all the English factories, Worcester played perhaps the leading part in making this Cinderella of the porcelain family. As the Chinese had found, cobalt was one of the easier pigments to manage in the kiln, so that by the time of Worcester's emergence, blue was a colour which had become popular on all classes of less expensive porcelain and earthenware. It was natural, therefore, that Worcester, with its keen eye on the growing public for fine wares at reasonable prices, should develop this branch strongly.

We have already looked at some of the blue-painted wares of the Bristol/Worcester days (see page 8): some of these are more scarce nowadays in blue than in their poly-chrome versions. These very earliest members of the Worcester blue and white race attract, not only by the delicate styles of their painting, but also by their fine potting. In some instances, as we have seen, it is of the 'eggshell' thinness which was the goal with some of the very finest of the Chinese porcelain wares.

Although as time went on the blue developed a wide range of hues, the painting around 1755 had a pale greyish tint. The early *chinoiserie* has already been discussed; later these blossomed out into great variety. The prunus blossom was much used, especially in association with the 'cracked ice' as seen in the original Chinese porcelain, where these two symbols stood for the breaking-up of Winter and the emergence of Spring. The tall willowy ladies who floated across the designs, sometimes with a small boy carrying a parasol before them became popularly known here as 'Long Elizas', a rough and ready translation by the English merchants of the Dutch shipmasters' *lange lijsen* (literally tall ladies.)

Another popular theme in blue, as well as in polychrome, is the 'hundred antiques', a collection of objects venerated by the Chinese which usually included—very much stylized —a jewel, a coin, books, a horn cup and an artemisia leaf: the word 'hundred' (*po-ku*) means 'many' rather than a specific number. There is much anglicizing in the naming of some of these patterns. A subject of Chinese warriors and jugglers is called the 'Eloping Bride' or 'Love Chase' pattern; another, showing a very Chinese dragon and soldier, has become known as 'St George and Dragon'. (There is, by the way, a 'Worcester Dragon', as distinct from the 'Broseley dragon' of Caughley.) A pattern with a tall fence, bamboo trees and rooks is called the 'Plantation'; while the famous Arita quail,

A coffee cup and two coffee cans, printed: (Above) *'The Tea Party'.* (Centre) *'The Fortune Teller'* (*Dr Wall*). c. *1760–5.* (Below) *Stippled printing of the Flight and Barr period* (*see p. 59*). (Harris Museum and Art Gallery, Preston.)

19

which appears on blue and white as well as in the famous Kakiemon colours (see colour plate), is also here called the 'partridge'.

Other well-known patterns include a zigzag fence with a rock and a peony; two swimming ducks and a bridge; a thick gnarled willow root; a bird perched on rushes with rocks and peonies; a cormorant with a man fishing. Blue and white includes, of course, printed blue and white; about which more will be said under that head.

The collector who likes a wide variety of shapes will perhaps do better here than anywhere else, for many more 'useful' wares were made in blue and white than in polychrome. Cups and saucers can be round or hexagonal, with several kinds of surface mouldings. There is a wavy pattern called the 'feather' (page 23), and another like a chrysanthemum. Several styles of ribbing or fluting (page 14) are seen, together with mouldings of floral scrolls, petals, etc. Plates are also to be found with some of these mouldings; and an especially attractive combination here (seen on page 43) is the basket-weave rim with a wavy edge, decorated with the work of the 'wet-brush' painter.

The moulded cabbage-leaf jugs for which Worcester is famous are very plentifully available in blue and white, often with the mask spout, as are also all the vine-leaf dessert and tiny pickle-dishes, pierced baskets, comports, salad bowls, soup tureens, butter-dishes, sauce-boats; there are even such items as knife and fork handles, knife rests, salt spoons, tea-caddy spoons and a pierced variety of the latter which are claimed to be egg-draining spoons. Tea jars take on several shapes, oval, round or square, sometimes with ribbed moulding; and teapots come in many shapes, some peculiar to Worcester, others of universal adoption. Among the ornamental wares may be mentioned flower-holders, cornucopias, and all kinds of vases and pots; among the 'useful' wares are candlesticks, eye-cups, spittoons and even chamber pots.

4. Transfer Printing

It was typical of Worcester enterprise that the factory should have moved very quickly into the newly invented business and art of transfer printing. The public which longed to be in the mode with *chinoiserie* after Pillement or flowers after Meissen, but could not afford the very expensive originals, were not at all averse to having 'china ware' decorated by a cheaper method. In transfer printing, therefore, Worcester found an even larger public—and incidentally made a new contribution to ceramics which was developed very strongly in the following century on Staffordshire earthenware.

Although there are claims for the invention of transfer printing at Liverpool by the creamware printers, Sadler and Green, it now seems to be generally conceded that the process first saw the light of day at York House, Battersea, home of the famous boxes—or at least of such as were not made in South Staffordshire! It was used at Battersea on enamels and also, there is good reason to believe, on porcelain made or brought from elsewhere—a contemporary writer describes the establishment as a 'china and enamel' factory.

The process involved engraving a design—original or from an existing print—upon a copper plate, and transferring it on inked paper to a piece of china or earthenware. By combining several transfers it is possible to build up designs on wares of almost any shape: where there are

Two-handled sauce-boat, with 'primitive' transfer printing and painted over in colours. c. 1756. 7½ in. long. (Victoria & Albert Museum.)

21

'May Day' mug, transfer printed in black. c. 1760. (Sotheby & Co.)

moulded surfaces (see page 21) panels can be 'reserved' for this purpose as blanks. The technique is said to have been invented by John Brooks, an Irish engraver working at Battersea, with the encouragement of the principal of the place, Stephen Janssen, who was a stationer and therefore would have known all about prints and inking processes.

Printing at Worcester, however, did not come to full perfection immediately, and there are 'primitives' in the field which are in some ways even more attractive than the later efforts. They include small landscapes and figures with what has been called a 'sooty' appearance, the enamel resting on the surface of the glaze. Nevertheless they have a charming delicacy of line and they appear on the sauceboats and creamers discussed on page 12. Some are single prints of small animals and birds, such as squirrels and pheasants, printed in oval frames, frequently surrounded by scrollwork and flowers in relief. There are also Chinese figure subjects, castles and rural views: inside the vessels are prints showing, for example, a milking scene and also the well-known 'bubbles' print, much used on later pieces. On charming two-handled sauce-boats (page 21) are to be found small designs illustrating *The Four Ages of Man* and *The Four Seasons*.

The consensus now is that these pieces were not made at Bristol at all—or if they were, the undecorated ones had been kept in stock for later use at Worcester—and that they represent Hancock's early attempts at printing with the Worcester glaze and enamels.

The Robert Hancock mentioned above, an important figure in Worcester history, was an original painter and engraver of high merit. Born in Burslem, Staffordshire, in about 1730, he was apprenticed to a Birmingham engraver. By 1753 he was working at Battersea in close association with Brooks and with Simon-François Ravenet, the French engraver, and the artist L. P. Boitard. It is not surprising, therefore, that his early work shows a strong French influence. He used subjects after Watteau, Boucher and Lancret and contributed prints to popular drawing-books like *The Ladies' Amusement*, *The Complete Drawing Master*, *The Artists' Vade Mecum*, etc. Many of these also appear on Worcester porcelain, as we shall see. By 1757 at least, perhaps a year earlier, Hancock was working at Worcester: this is testified by the date of his engraving of Frederick the Great on the well-known 'King of Prussia' mugs and plates, adapted from the painting by Antoine Pesne (page 26). Hancock took with him to Worcester the copperplates which he had used at both Battersea and Bow.

The Worcester factory were extremely proud of their

Cream jug printed with the 'L'Amour' pattern; plate impressed with 'feather' pattern and printed with a classical landscape; teacup and saucer with the 'Milkmaid' pattern. (All Victoria & Albert Museum.)

transfer printing as shown in such work as this—indeed they had every right to be, for its quality has never been surpassed anywhere. Their 'jet-enamelled' black is still as fresh and alive as on the day it was printed, and the lilac is especially attractive, having the habit of sinking into the glaze and so acquiring great depth. There is also some reddish brown printing which has been much admired. The prints were often accompanied by plain black bands on rims, or a border pattern. It could also be combined with gilding or painting in enamel colours, also in reserved panels or pieces painted with the famous coloured grounds (see page 34).

Vase painted with the 'birds and overturned basket' pattern from The Ladies' Amusement. (Sotheby & Co.)

Apart from his French subjects, Hancock also used a great many of the *chinoiseries* mentioned on page 22, in particular designs by Jean Pillement, the French decorator, who was working in London at this time, much of whose work appeared in a book of engravings called the *Livre de Chinois* by P. C. Canot. He also drew upon famous English artists such as Reynolds, Gainsborough, Luke Sullivan and Francis Hayman.

Many pieces bear Hancock's initials or full signature in various forms, and this has sometimes caused confusion with another person at Worcester having the same initials, Richard Holdship. He was the brother of Josiah Holdship, one of the original proprietors, and it has been thought that when the initials 'R.H.' occur together with an anchor, notably on an indubitable Hancock design called 'L'Amour' (see page 23), the anchor symbol is used as a rebus for (or pun on) Holdship's name. On the famous 'King of

Prussia' mug there is not only the R.H. and the anchor, but also, very inconspicuously on the flowing ribbon at the back, *R. Hancock fecit. Worcester*, as though the engraver was trying to leave his authorship of the famous design in no doubt.

That Richard Holdship did have some connection with engraving or printing at Worcester is shown by the fact that when he left there for Derby in 1759 to instruct that factory in the art of transfer printing, he used his initials, the anchor and the word 'Derby', on engravings he made for Duesbury, the proprietor of the Derby factory. That there was also rivalry between the two 'R.H.'s' is shown by some lines published in *The Gentleman's Magazine* in December, 1757, called *On seeing an armed bust of the King of Prussia curiously imprinted on a Porcelain Cup of the Worcester manufacture with the Emblem of his Victories*:

> What praise, ingenious Holdship! is thy due,
> Who first on porcelain the fair portrait drew!
> Who first alone to full perfection brought,
> The curious art, by rival numbers sought.

A month later, there appeared in *Berrow's Worcester Journal* a slightly different rendering of these verses which acknowledges that Holdship "the art designed" but gives full credit to Hancock for his part in the engraving:

> Hancock, my friend, don't *grieve*, tho' Holdship has the praise,
> 'Tis yours to execute, 'tis his to wear the bays.

Mr Cyril Cook in his *Life and Work of Robert Hancock*, an invaluable guide to the engraver's work, comes to the conclusion that when Hancock used the initials he was trying to establish his part in introducing transfer printing at Worcester, but that he added his full name where he desired to assert his own part in the actual engraving.

Two of Hancock's most popular designs are shown on the coffee cups from the collection at the Harris Museum and Art Gallery, Preston (see page 19) and these, incidentally, demonstrate an economical way of collecting Old

'King of Prussia' mug, transfer printed in black, with the Holdship anchor rebus and signed by the engraver Robert Hancock. (Victoria & Albert Museum.)

Worcester patterns, for no pieces are to be picked up so cheaply as coffee cups. The Museum has published a book-let illustrating its collection. 'The Fortune Teller' is a famous and early design, and is from a drawing originally by Boitard, with whom, as already noted, Hancock worked at Battersea.

'The Tea Party' appears in at least three versions—the original has not so far been traced—usually showing Hancock's initials or signature.

Another of these patterns, 'L'Amour' (see page 23), was taken from a design of C. N. Cochin *fils* of about 1745, and various versions have typical Hancock additions such as a 'Neptune' fountain, a garden roller, and a dog.

The 'May Day' mug on page 22 depicts a charming custom of eighteenth-century life, whereby on the first day of May a party of milkmaids, all dressed in their gayest finery, would go round from door to door with a 'garland' of silver plate decked out with flowers of the season.

A quite different style is shown in the well-known engraving of birds and an overturned basket of fruit (page 24), but it is apparently Hancock's own work, for it appears in *The Ladies' Amusement* signed *R. Hancock sculp*: it was also used on Staffordshire enamels and Liverpool porcelain.

A change in the proprietorship of the factory in 1772 saw the going of the Holdships, father and son, and the acceptance of Hancock as a partner, but two or three years later, after some disputes with his colleagues, Hancock sold out his share for £6,000. In spite of losing much of his savings in a bank crash, he seems to have gone on to lead a busy and prosperous life, engraving, drawing and painting, specializing much in portraits, showing at the Royal Academy, and publishing fine work in books. He died in 1817 in his eighty-eighth year at Brislington, near Bristol, onetime home of some of the finest of our painted delftware.*

Transfer-printed wares which have been painted over with enamels, or had enamelling added on borders, are very likely the work of James Giles, the outside decorator, of whom we shall be hearing more later. He bought several services of 'jet-enamelled' porcelain at the Worcester sales of 1769. This work is quite different, however, from a class of wares which has Chinese figures—usually the 'Red Ox' pattern—and which is printed in brown outline and has the pattern filled in with washes of colour: there may also be borders printed in underglaze blue.

Only a few pieces of overglaze-printing at Worcester bear a mark. Occasionally the crossed swords of Dresden with figures like 9 and 91 are found, also the incised scratched cross (page 16). The seal and the 'W' mark appear rarely, while on some pieces, made from early

* See *Delftware* in this series.

copperplates used again in the Flight and Barr period, the scratched or incised 'B' may be found.

UNDERGLAZE BLUE PRINTING

By far the largest class of Worcester transfer-printed wares —or indeed of any Worcester available plentifully to the collector today—is that printed on the 'biscuit' under the glaze. The practice seems to have started about 1760; it must certainly have been known at Worcester by 1764, when Richard Holdship went to Derby, for it was this process that he introduced there. By this time, of course, Worcester was in full spate with its coloured wares, and printing on the 'biscuit' was obviously a cheaper line intended for the middle-class trade. Only blue was used, and because of the tendency for the pigment to spread, a less refined style of engraving was used. There are a few examples of adaptation of Hancock's designs used in overglaze printing, but for the most part the underglaze patterns consist of flowers and conventionalized landscapes. There was, apparently, a strike among the painters in 1770, in protest, as it has been conjectured, against this further mechanization of their work.

Nevertheless, these wares have the usual Worcester virtues of fine body and glaze, of good craftsmanship and taste. They do not live happily alongside overglaze wares, but, like the painted wares, they do like each other's company, and a few shelves of them make a fine show when judiciously chosen for shapes.

5. Worcester 'Japans'

In 1769 the Company held two public auctions of their wares. With the second of these, held at Christie's, a catalogue was issued which named a whole range of 'Japan' patterns. It has been possible to identify some of these, and collectors have been fascinated to trace the origins of some of the motifs used. They often come from the most unexpected places, as we shall see.

There were two main influences, the earliest of which had its origin in the delicate and restrained patterns from Arita named after the Japanese potter Kakiemon, whose family worked in that centre from about 1650 to 1720. The Kakiemons used brilliant opaque blue, transparent yellow, blue-green and a yellow-green, brick red and gold. There was usually a central motif of flowers, animals or birds perched on or beside a tree, with a narrow floral or diaper border.

Here were the origins of Worcester's 'fine old wheatsheaf', 'Japan' and 'partridge' (colour plate) patterns, first imitated at Meissen and then at Bow before arriving on Severnside. In using these names, nobody worries very much that the 'wheatsheaf' is actually a banded hedge and the 'partridge' a quail, or that there was one painter who

Worcester 'Japan' patterns: (Left) Sugar bowl stand with 'old mosaic Japan' pattern. c. 1760. (Centre) Plate with 'Queen's' or 'whorl' pattern. c. 1780. 7⅝ in. (Right) Dessert dish with the 'Bengal Tyger' pattern. c. 1780. (All Victoria & Albert Museum.)

Cream jug, painted in colours with the 'fine old Japan' pattern. c. 1770. $5\frac{3}{8}$ in. (Victoria & Albert Museum.)

gave his quails a pronounced hump-back: he seems to have worked at Bow as well as Worcester.

If the Worcester painters never quite achieved the exquisite asymmetrical balance of the Japanese, they certainly followed the originals in showing off the fine white body of the porcelain. As a variation, however, they also used borders and scattered flowers in the Kakiemon style on a class of yellow-ground pieces with *chinoiserie* and landscapes painted in red in shaped panels. The work of this 'painter of the Chinese landscapes' is also to be found on blue and white.

With the rest of their 'Japans', Worcester went into reverse and seemed to be doing their level best to hide the porcelain of which they were so proud—in fact to disguise it as something else. Here the model was again taken from Arita, but in a later style which the local potters had developed mainly for the export trade to Europe. It was now called Imari, after the port of shipment. Both paste and potting of these wares were inferior to Kakiemon's, but this was concealed by using heavy patterns copied from the rich colourful mosaics of Chinese and Japanese brocaded silks and lacquer. Outstanding amongst the colours was a dark underglaze blue, with much gilding and red enamelling. These wares were not at all in the Japanese taste, but as eighteenth-century delicacy moved towards nineteenth-century ostentation they became immensely popular in Europe for their very richness and elaboration.

At Worcester, however, the Imari patterns underwent a remarkable sea-change. Such oriental motifs as the imperial dragon, the stork, the phoenix or ho-ho bird, also the bamboo, peony, chrysanthemum and prunus blossom, were all used indiscriminately, and sometimes translated into the sheerest fantasy. Exact copies were few, and any Chinese or Japanese used to reading a significance into the motifs would have been bewildered by the products of Worcester. Whenever they felt inspired to do so the Worcester men mixed together Meissen flowers, Chinese mosaics or scales, Japanese diaper, or in fact anything which served their turn and which was likely to tickle the public palate for decorated china.

At the time these 'Japans' were made, the Worcester versions were often vastly more attractive than the originals from which they were copying, for the Japanese and Chinese wares then coming to this country were of the relatively inferior export types: those in the more subtle taste of the orientals themselves were as yet hardly known here.

One of the most popular of the 'Japans' was the Catalogue's 'Old Japan fan', seen here on our cream jug (page 30). This is directly copied 'brocaded Imari', being made up of half-chrysanthemums with petals diversely painted in red, blue, green and gold projecting fanwise from the base and the neck. There are three dark blue discs on the body with gilt trellis diaper, and two more on the cover—which, coming from Worcester, has a thoroughly English flower knop painted in natural colours.

A wide range of patterns has panels which radiate out

(Left to right) *Teacup and saucer with Imari pattern. Mark a fretted square in blue. c. 1770. Coffee-pot with sprays of prunus blossom and conventional flowering plants in colours and gold. c. 1760. Mark, fretted square in blue. 8½ in. high. Cup and saucer with the 'Sir Joshua Reynolds' pattern. c. 1770.* (All Victoria & Albert Museum.)

from a central motif, and one of the finest and richest of these is evidently what the Catalogue calls 'Old Mosaick Japan'. This is seen in our oval dish (page 29). In the centre is a blossoming prunus-bough bent around on itself, and from this extend eight panels in a radiating design with Japan flowers in three of them; others have, respectively, a swastika pattern and a flower in gilt on blue, a lozenge design and swastika in blue, a large lozenge in blue, red and gold, and another with lozenge and flowers in pink and yellow. The formal lines of the panels are broken by chrysanthemum heads in reserve. Two other versions of these radiating panels are seen in the cups and saucers on page 31, one of them showing the ho-ho bird or phoenix on a tree stump, a motif in what is known as the 'Sir Joshua Reynolds' pattern.

From the colours named in this account, it will be seen how rich these patterns are. That Worcester thought them worthy imitations of the original is shown by the fact that plates with this pattern often bear the mock-Chinese character marks (see page 63).

The first of the two 'Queen's' patterns at Worcester, sometimes called the 'whorl', the spiral or the 'Catherine wheel', looks like a 'Japan', but it has been held that the oriental versions of it are, in fact, later in date than those of Worcester. They may well have been copied in China from the work of some orientally inspired painter living and working at Worcester. This kind of cross-fertilization went on a great deal.

As shown on page 29, the pattern has spiral bands with counterchanged blue and white designs enriched with motifs in coloured enamels. These motifs remind one of those on Paisley shawls, the design for which, incidentally, was taken from Kashmir and also appears on Persian faience. This 'whorl' pattern continued in use well into the Flight and Barr days, when another 'Queen's' pattern, the 'Royal Lily', was named for Queen Charlotte when she visited the factory.

'Japans' figure among the patterns named after well-known people who had bought services or had them made. The 'Bodenham' is an early scale-blue with lively Chinese figures in reversed panels. The 'Kempthorne' is of an unusually restrained design, with stylized foliage and flowers nicely placed. A service painted with it was given by the factory to a Renatus Kempthorne of Mullion, Cornwall, in return for hospitality to one of the Worcester principals when he was in the district searching for a new vein of soaprock.

The brilliant colours of the *famille verte*, one of the great 'families' of Chinese porcelain, appear here rather less brilliantly, especially in the 'Bishop Sumner' service, which has a kylin, the Chinese mythical monster, surrounded by border panels with rocks, flowering plants and various other mythical beasts.

Pierced-work basket with wavy rim, painted with chinoiserie. c. *1765.* *15⅛ in. long.* (Victoria & Albert Museum.)

6. Coloured Grounds

Outstanding among all the Worcester achievements are the famous coloured grounds, sometimes plain, sometimes patterned in various ways. They are often enriched with gilding, and provide apt and beautiful settings for painting in reserved panels.

In developing these grounds Worcester was probably most influenced by Chelsea, but their true origin is Meissen. The Saxon factory had tried its hand at many of the ground colours used in the eighteenth century long before porcelain was made in England, and had brought most of them to high perfection. These grounds were also used at Sèvres, with interesting and beautiful variations.

In the English factories, because of the very imperfections of the soft-paste and the lead-glaze, the colours became transformed into something much richer and more alive than those in continental hard-paste. Worcester, in particular, brought to it the fine discipline of its craftsmanship and the reticence of its forms. It also offered as its own special contribution a range of reticulated, scaled and

'Celestial-blue' ground teapot, with reserved panels painted by the James Giles 'cut-fruit' painter. 6 in. high. Crossed swords mark. (Sotheby & Co.)

Honey-pot and ladle painted with flowers in reserved panels with gilt lacework borders on a scale-blue ground. (British Museum.)

diapered patterns on the various coloured grounds.

No catalogue survives from the first of the sales held in 1769 but an advertisement in the *Public Advertiser* described the goods offered. There were 'Table and Dessert Services, Leaves, Compotiers, Tea and Coffee Equipages, Baskets, Vases, Perfume Pots, Jars, Beakers, Cisterns, Tureens, Porringers, Bowls, etc.' These were set out 'in the beautiful colours of Mazarine Blue and Gold, Sky-blue, Pea-green, French-green, Sea-green, Purple, Scarlet and other Variety of Colours, richly decorated with chased and burnished gold; and many other Articles both useful and ornamental. The whole enamelled in the highest Taste, and curiously painted in Figures, Birds, Landscapes, Flowers, Fruits, etc.'

One of the earliest grounds to be used was the 'powder-blue', originated by the Chinese who produced the mottled effect by blowing pigment through a tube covered with gauze at one end. At Worcester the colouring oxide was sprinkled on to the ground as a dry powder, so melting in tiny points of colour against the white background.

The 'mazarine-blue' of the advertisement was once thought to have been powder-blue, but it now seems to have been Worcester's attempt—not an outstandingly successful one—to emulate the *gros bleu* used at Sèvres and very well imitated at Chelsea. Another early colour used at Worcester was yellow, while 'pea-green' is perhaps the modern 'apple-green', a colour which, incidentally, would not in its eighteenth-century formulation take gilding directly applied.

35

'Scarlet' is thought to have been 'claret'; and Mr W. B. Honey believed that on the close of that factory, the workman responsible for this colour at Chelsea migrated not to Derby, as did most of the staff, but to Worcester. The colour was not much used, for it was difficult to get right: modern forgers have remedied this deficiency by applying it sparingly to decorated but perfectly genuine pieces, thus making the deception exceedingly difficult to detect. The 'purple' was probably our 'maroon' and the 'sky-blue' our 'turquoise', another much-forged ground colour. Although there are all-over grounds of this and the claret, they appear most often as cornucopia-shaped borders richly gilt.

Artists of all ages have been faced with the problem of making a coloured surface more interesting by breaking it up in some way and yet retaining the broad effect of the coloured ground. One frequently used motif is the scale or imbrication, perhaps suggested by the scales of a fish, the overlapping feathers of birds, the tiles of a roof, or the waves of the seashore. At Worcester, possibly acting on a hint from the *mosaik* of Meissen and Berlin, or maybe from some Lambeth delftware based on a Chinese original, this was developed into what must be regarded as an original creation in ceramics.

It appears in two forms, the earlier having larger scales—the 'Bodenham' service is an example—brushed on to a blue underglaze. The later style had smaller scales.

The blue fish-scale usually points upwards, but the overglaze pink 'peacock' scale points both upwards and downwards. This was used at Meissen between 1740 and 1760, and also at Chelsea. The brick-red scale is rare, as is the pink. Worcester used another method of breaking up the ground, with diapers of tiny circles resembling shagreen —the Chinese 'fishroe'. The hint may have been taken by Worcester direct from China or through the intermediary of the *mosaik* patterns of Meissen and Berlin, which were very much used about the time that Worcester were developing their grounds.

The 'Lady Mary Wortley-Montagu' service shows another skilled way of breaking up a scale-blue ground. Flower-sprays in gilding cover the ground, and there are reserved rococo panels with birds and flowers.

FIGURE PAINTING

Much painting on coloured-ground pieces was done by artists in the studio of James Giles, the London decorator. Another freelance, who worked for several factories, was Jeffrey Hamet O'Neale, who had a studio in Oxford Road, London, but was working in Worcester from 1768 to 1770. Many of his figure and landscape paintings appear in heart-shaped panels reserved in the coloured grounds, notably on large vases. He seems to have made a speciality of horses, which he did with a characteristic touch readily recognizable (see colour plate).

Another of the rare figure painters working on Worcester porcelain at this time was James Donaldson, a miniaturist from Edinburgh. His figure painting is usually in the manner of Boucher: the vase on the colour plate shows an example of his flower painting, which was very accomplished.

Heart-shaped fruit dish, painted in the style of the Sèvres bird painters Evans and Aloncle. c. 1775. 11¼ in. long. (Victoria & Albert Museum.)

7. Worcester Birds

Hardly less renowned than the fruit and flowers, and even the Japans, are the Worcester birds. They range from sedate, naturalistic creatures to the wildest and most fantastic.

Collectors have found the usual interest in classifying these birds and in trying to identify their painters. Only rarely is the actual name known, and for the most part the different hands of these artists can be discerned only from the style and types of their birds and the other painting which accompanies them.

To begin with, the birds were oriental. There were the Kakiemon quails in the 'partridge' pattern (see the colour plate), also the slender, long-tailed birds of 'the fine-brush painter' who perhaps worked at Bristol. There are similar ones once thought to have been by Michael Edkins.

From about 1755 several types of birds begin to make their appearance. One painter, responsible for a mug inscribed with the name of Lord Sandys (Dr Wall's guardian) and the date 1759, and of the great armorial jug shown on the colour plate, also painted a good many characteristic birds, notably an owl on a branch being mobbed by other birds.

A little before the full flush of the exotic bird painting, while the factory was still under the influence of Meissen, there are some naturalistic birds taken from the Saxon factory, which presumably copied them from engravings, as they did in the case of their flower paintings. The birds are rather stiffly drawn, but the designs are nicely set out and make the most of white porcelain; in this respect they remind one rather of Kakiemon designs.

Sèvres styles in this genre came in fairly early at Worcester with some birds from the hand of a painter who seems either to have worked at Sèvres or to have been very much under the influence of painters there such as Evans and Aloncle. These birds here are well-fed, long-legged creatures, presented in a watery landscape, with smaller birds in flight all around. The subject was apparently used at Chelsea, and there are versions of it in two rather different hands, one of them being shown (page 37) in the Victoria & Albert Museum's dish; the other appears on a piece of the same shape in the British Museum. Collectors know this as the 'Lord Rodney' service.

The 'cut-fruit' painter already noted was also responsible for the famous 'dishevelled birds', a name these creatures owe to Mr Hobson, which, as he truly said, have a 'wild and dissipated air'. They certainly are weird creatures, with feathers awry, and usually looking apprehensively around them: they have also been called 'agitated birds'. They are to be seen in the panels of the 'Lady Mary Wortley-Montagu' service (page 42).

Another artist, sometimes called the 'Chelsea painter', used, in Mr Honey's phrase, a 'full wet brush'; that he also is to be identified with the Giles studio is claimed on the grounds of the similarity of his style to the well-known 'Grubbe' plates, which were handed down in the Giles family and are now at the Victoria & Albert Museum. His lively work is to be seen on the plate with the basket-weave rim (page 43).

Chocolate or caudle cup and cover, painted with birds in reserved panels on a blue ground striped with gold. Mark, an open crescent. c. 1778–80. (British Museum.)

39

Another painter has a bird with ringed staring eyes, as seen in the caudle or chocolate cup on page 39. Here there is a peacock on the pot and a guinea fowl on the stand, with other birds on the cover, all in reserved panels on a blue ground. Gold striping like this is seen more often on Chelsea-Derby than Worcester. The body and tail of these birds have a characteristic S-curve and the painter makes much use of red foliage. The style was copied at Liverpool and used earlier at Longton Hall, perhaps from the same engravings.

Another painter employs what has been called a 'smudgy' brush-stroke, without the dots used so often by the others. The foliage around them is coarse and thickly drawn, the birds themselves having great goitred necks. There is also a bird painter who gives both the S-form and the staring eyes to his birds, but makes particular use of the 'dry-blue' enamel for plumage.

A named painter—if still unresolved conjecture about his name and his identity is to be called naming—was a certain Monsieur Soqui (or Saqui or Lequoi), said to have been 'an excellent painter and enameller from Sèvres'. His birds are proud and stately, with out-thrust breasts, and he uses the same kind of shadowy background as the Evans and Aloncle painter (page 37) with strong colours and thick stippling which gives the birds' plumage the appearance of being slightly ruffled.

8. Flowers and Fruit

Flower painting appeared on wares at Worcester from the very earliest days, and at first tended to follow the oriental styles seen in the Japans. The next important influence was Meissen. There are several quite distinct styles, beginning with the *deutsche Blumen* or *Streu-blumen*, which were small bouquets and scattered sprigs, painted in semi-naturalistic style. There were also the *Meissner Blumen*, where the flowers are idealized and arranged in formal bouquets.

One painter placed a single bloom in a bouquet of smaller ones, as seen in the 'Blind Earl' plate on page 52 and the coffee-pot on page 31. Another had a characteristic set of flowers which he festooned across reserved panels with light chains, as seen in the honey-pot on page 35. This piece is also interesting for the panels with the shapes of mirrors and vases edged with gilt rococo scrollwork, and also for the gilt lacework borders on the neck. There are two broth-bowls in the Frank Lloyd collection at the British Museum with similar flowers. By contrast another flower painter spread his blooms all over the surface, in a manner much more popular in late Victorian times.

The Meissen flowers were often accompanied by fruit and vegetables, some of them cut or sliced. One artist in particular favoured large 'spotted' fruit, filbert nuts, berries, radishes and the like. Some of these types were at one time thought to be the work of a painter who came to Worcester from Meissen by way of Chelsea, for it seemed that his hand could be detected on pieces from all three places. It is now believed, however, that he may have worked at the studio of an outside decorator, like James Giles (page 37), painting wares bought 'in the white' by his employer from both Chelsea and Worcester, and that he directly copied some Meissen pieces.

Plate of the 'Lady Mary Wortley Montagu' pattern, with 'dishevelled birds' in panels reserved on a ground of scale blue with floral sprays overlaid in gold (Victoria & Albert Museum.)

The Meissen influence is also to be seen in the ribbed teapot in the Victoria & Albert Museum, from the Catalogue of 1769, where it is advertised in a set as 'twelve ribb'd handle cups and saucers, six coffee cups, teapot and stand, basin and plate, sugar dish, cover and plate, tea jar and spoon boat, enamell'd in parrots'. It is painted in enamel colours with gilding, and the neck and the lid have a border of a close floral pattern in the old Japan style with gilt edges. Collectors who wonder why there always seem to be

Dessert dish of the 'Hope Edwardes' service painted in natural colours, and with conventional floral sprays in gold on a claret border edged with gilt scrolls. c. 1770. 7⅞ in. wide. (Victoria & Albert Museum.)

more coffee and tea cups about than saucers will note here one of the reasons: that only one set of saucers served for both coffee and tea: and why not, when one comes to think of it?

While on the subject of sets one may note the very pleasant *déjeuner* service (see page 51), where the fruit and flower painting with butterflies is joined by the then newly fashionable Neo-classical urn.

Next among the influences at Worcester was Sèvres. From the very beginning the great ideal on Severnside had been the creamy white paste of the Paris factory, its fine painting and the rich coloured grounds glowing up through the glaze. Somewhere about 1770, no doubt with the advent of the painters of Chelsea, many themes were taken more directly from La Pompadour's private porcelain factory.

They appear most obviously in the well-known 'trellis' or 'hop-pole' patterns—called 'French Flowers' at Worcester —which appear in a number of variations; some of them are shown on page 44.

The tea jar has ribbed sides, and there are four triple

Openwork basket in a Sèvres style from the 'Earl Manvers' service. c. 1775. (British Museum.)

Cup and saucer and tea jar painted with versions of the Sèvres 'hop trellis' pattern in colours and gilding, borders of turquoise diapered with black scale pattern. Teapot in Sèvres style, with 'dry-blue' flowers painted over a background striped with bands of gilt C-scrolls. 6½ in. high. (All British Museum.)

standards of hop poles with festoons between. The borders are turquoise with a black scale diaper pattern and gilt edging. The form here is very pleasant and is obviously from the Orient. With the coffee cup and saucer, which are also reeded and fluted, the pattern places three uprights in red, bound with a gilt band, between alternating festoons of leaves and berries. The borders are in *bleu de roi*, with formal gilt patterns and edge. It is marked with a thin gold crescent.

A further variation is seen in the attractive dessert basket (page 43) with pierced sides and twisted handles in basket-work. On the outside are the rosette attachments in natural colours so often seen on the Worcester baskets. The oval medallion in the centre shows a bunch of plums, and radiating compartments have a border of pink scrolls festooned with hops. This design continues right up and round the openwork of the sides, which is bordered with pink trellis pattern, broken by gilt scrolls enclosing hops. This pattern is from the 'Earl Manvers' service.

Another characteristic Sèvres style is seen in the teapot on page 44, where the background is striped with bands of gilt C-scrolls framed by double lines leading to a border of scrolls on the neck: over this are floated bouquets and detached sprays of flowers in the so-called 'dry blue' (colour plate), a particularly brilliant blue enamel once thought to be unique to Worcester, but now demonstrated by Mr George Savage to have been used also in the Giles studio. It often appears on its own in a quite different kind of 'blue and white'.

Pleasant flower painting is also seen in some other pieces shown here, especially on the colour plate. The spoon tray on page 53 has a landscape in a medallion with turquoise lustre and gilt rim and flower sprays within a royal blue and gilt border. The landscape itself was once attributed to a painter known as 'Fogo', but this personage is now considered to be a fiction.

Sprays of old English garden flowers, with detached blossoms, are seen in the vine-leaf dish made from two overlapping leaves with green serrated edges (page 52): the piece has a brown 'rustic' handle and a stout triangular footrim.

Scalloped edge plate with basketweave rim and painted with birds on fruit tree branches by 'wet-brush' painter. c. 1770. 8 in. diameter. (Victoria & Albert Museum.)

45

9. Armorial Wares

The eighteenth century saw a great vogue for the decoration of porcelain with armorial bearings. Enormous sets were commissioned through the dealers, mainly from China. In the antiques trade, these wares have acquired the name 'Armorial Lowestoft', owing to a peculiar misapprehension on the part of a nineteenth-century ceramic historian named Chaffers. He supposed that because the Chinese had imitated some Lowestoft patterns, all these great heraldic services, made of indubitable hard-paste Chinese porcelain, had been potted—or at least decorated—at a small, short-lived soft-paste factory on the Suffolk coast.

Some of the English factories did make armorial porcelain, but often only as replacements for Chinese sets, or as single pieces, intended for presentation. But full services were made as well and Worcester started as early as about 1755. Mr H. Rissik Marshall gathered together an exhaustive list of these, based largely upon his own collection.

The arms usually appear in association with all the other motifs to be found on Worcester porcelain, according, one supposes, to the fancy of the customers. In the early days the bearings were set in rococo shields, and sometimes these were 'stilted', that is to say, set up on rococo legs perhaps in a landscape, or they might also float in mid-air against a country view, when the effect is almost surrealistic.

One of the most magnificent specimens, not only of heraldic porcelain, but of Worcester production of any kind, is the great jug shown on the colour plate which bears the arms of Collis with Barrow in pretence, against a Meissen-like landscape with figures. It is by the 'painter of the Lord Sandys mug' (see page 38), and the landscape painted all around it includes a lake scene, a bridge and distant ships and buildings. After about 1760 the escutcheons tended to

46

be put against plain white grounds, with simple decorative sprays and formal designs.

Punchbowls were favourite pieces for armorial decoration. From about the year 1766 comes our fine specimen (page 47) from the collection brought together from all over Europe by Lady Charlotte Schreiber, now displayed in the Victoria & Albert Museum. Lady Charlotte bought it in London about the same time as the yellow-ground dish mentioned on page 49. 'Button bought me a wonderfully fine Worcester deep dish or bowl, with the arms of the Elys on it,' she writes in her *Journal*, 'it is a noble piece, and though I had to pay dear for it (£20), I am very glad to have it to add to the collection.' One wonders what the piece would make if it came on the market today.

The arms are those of Nicholas Loftus, second Earl of Ely of the first creation, who succeeded to the title in 1766. The ground is a dark powder blue, and scalloped sides are decorated with gilt scrollwork. The arms are in full colours, and the mark is a fretted square in blue.

Armorial punchbowl, painted in colours and gilt, with dark scale-blue ground. c. 1770. (Victoria & Albert Museum.)

10. Moulding and Modelling

So far—except for the early moulded wares in silver style mentioned on page 15—we have been looking at Worcester in terms of decoration by painting and printing. The factory was not, as a rule, highly original in its forms, usually being content to accept those invented elsewhere, notably in China. But the modelled baskets and shaped dishes are deservedly famous, and are among the most attractive of the Worcester porcelain wares.

One of the most sought-after types is that shown on page 49, the outsides of which are moulded with a basket pattern enclosing quatrefoil flowers, the covers and sides being pierced. In the centre of the cover is a panel of openwork trellis pattern with small blossoms at the angles. The twig handles have flower and foliage attachments where they meet the cover. The basket patterns are lightly touched with pink and yellow and the formal reliefs are all in natural colours.

A more familiar type, perhaps, also on page 49, is a shaped oval form with a wavy rim. The sides in this piece are pierced in imitation of wickerwork, with flowers applied at the intersections. The handles, in the form of vine stems, bear leaves and bunches of grapes in relief, while the stand has a moulded edge and two shell handles. Basket and stand are painted round the inside with a border of diaper and floral ornament in the Chinese style, while the bottom of the basket features a bunch of conventional fruit in the Giles manner.

Another kind of piercing is seen in the basket (page 33) with the scalloped rim, which has leaves in relief on the outside and stands on a spreading foot. It is tipped up to show the painting in underglaze blue of a Chinese-style landscape, with buildings and boats on a lake. On both sides are sprays

Basket and stand with applied decoration, printed and painted in underglaze blue. c. 1770. 10¾ in. long. (Victoria & Albert Museum.)

of flowers and insects, and there are floral borders on the rim and above the foot. This was one of the types which was once thought to be Bow, but has since been re-attributed after analysis showed that it contained soapstone in the Worcester proportions.

Another of Lady Charlotte Schreiber's finds is shown below, bought when, according to her published *Journal* for 24 November 1884, she 'took a fancy' to a yellow-ground openwork Worcester dish. It is moulded with openwork scrolls and wickerwork pattern and pierced with four panels of open trellis work. The central panel, surrounded by crimson scrolls, is painted in colours with exotic birds among bushes.

(Left) Basket and stand with pierced wickerwork and applied flowers. c. 1765. Stand 10¾ in. long. (British Museum.) (Right) Canary-yellow openwork dish with moulded basketwork and open trellis work, painted with crimson scrolls and a panel of 'dishevelled birds'. c. 1770. 10⅝ in. long. (Victoria & Albert Museum.)

(Left) *Sugar basin and cover from the 'Lord Stormont' service with festoons of turquoise-blue drapery and a gilt fringe.* (Victoria & Albert Museum.) (Above) *Chamber candlestick, decorated in underglaze blue enamel colour and gilding. c. 1770–80. 6 in. diameter. Square mark.* (British Museum.)

Another class of ware once denied to Worcester, and quite recently restored, is a family of cauliflower tureens modelled in two parts, the leaves being edged with pale turquoise green (*below*). They are indeed very like Chelsea versions which they were once thought to be, but a typical Worcester touch will be noted in the transfer printing in black of moths and butterflies. An example of this, mentioned by Mr Barrett, has the transfer print painted over in colours.

Yet another type which has been transferred from Bow (page 15), is the cornucopia-shaped flower-holder shown here (*below*). Flat at the back, so that it can be hung on the wall, its front is moulded with a landscape featuring cattle and buildings. At the lower end are floral sprays moulded in relief or painted in blue, while beneath the everted scalloped rim is a border of foliated scrolls in relief above a band of floral and diaper ornament in blue. It bears the dagger mark. The Schreiber collection also has a pair of flower-holders in Staffordshire saltglaze taken from a similar mould.

(Left) *Cauliflower dish, printed with butterflies. Stand 6¾ in. Dr Wall period.* (Sotheby & Co.) (Right) *Cornucopia-shaped flower-holder, relief moulded, and painted in underglaze blue. Dagger mark. c. 1775. 8½ in. high.* (Victoria & Albert Museum.)

Famous among the Worcester wares are all the moulded trays and small dishes, usually in the form of leaves, sometimes overlapping. I have assembled a few of them on page 52 to show something of their range. One shows flower painting over a version of the so-called 'Blind Earl's' pattern, named after an Earl of Coventry. Below the painting are relief mouldings of leaves: on some variations these also are painted. Actually the Earl in question did not go blind until 1780, well after the introduction of this pattern; but this anachronism is not unusual with named patterns at Worcester: the 'Lady Mary Wortley Montagu' pattern, for example, was introduced several years after that lady's death.

The tiny pickle-tray, on 'eggshell' porcelain, bears some of the 'primitive' printing mentioned on page 22. The subject is 'The Flute Lesson', showing a boy teaching a girl how to play a flute, and it is based on a painting called *Le Maître Galant*, painted by Nicholas Lancret about the year 1743, and now in the palace of Fontainebleau.

The vine-leaf dish uses a palette of soft colours with a posy including a rose and a convolvulus, apparently the work of the artist sometimes known as the 'large bloom' painter (see page 41); there are also insects in flight and other sprays. The ground is white and the rustic handle green. A double version of the vine leaf, one overlapping the

Déjeuner set, with fluted moulding, painted with fruit, flowers and urn themes. (Victoria & Albert Museum.)

other, is seen in the next dish, whose painting of a spray of old English garden flowers and detached blossoms has already been noted. A snail lurks near the brown 'rustic' handle.

A mysterious personage known as 'Mr Tebo', is said to have been at Worcester some time in the 1770's. His work, with elaborate applied flowers, seems utterly un-Worcester-like, and some outside influence must surely have been brought to bear upon the managers to make them depart so far from their usual restraint. His mark was 'To' and it appears first on Bow figures, which were regarded as the work of a 'Mr Tebo' referred to by Josiah Wedgwood in his correspondence as having worked for him and being an incompetent modeller. This would not necessarily have meant that he was a bad 'repairer' or assembler of limbs on a figure.

Mr Honey thought the name might be an Anglicized form of Thibault: there were many French craftsmen working in England at that time. The 'To' mark appears again

a. Vine-leaf, painted in soft colours with a posy of roses and convolvulus by the 'large bloom' painter. 7½ in. b. Ivy-leaf pickle-tray with early 'transitional' print of 'The Flute Lesson'. c. 1756. 3¾ in. c. Double vine-leaf dish painted with old English garden flowers. 9½ in. d. 'Blind Earl's' pattern painted over with flowers. 6¼ in. All Dr Wall period. (Sotheby & Co.)

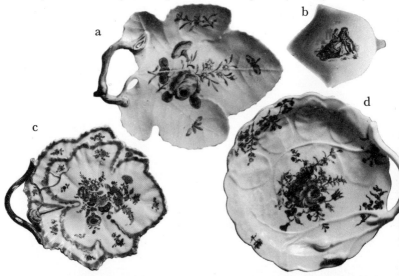

on the Plymouth hard-paste porcelain on intricately modelled shell and coral salts. Some baskets at Worcester have the mark embossed, which suggests that in this respect he was the modeller as well as the 'repairer'. On the other hand, Mr F. Rathbone, in his *Old Wedgwood*, made the interesting suggestion that 'To' could mean that the piece was fired 'top of the oven', as TBO can be an instruction to put the piece in the top of the biscuit oven.

For want of any better place, one might also mention here the pleasant little chamber candlestick (page 50) with which one of Worcester's eighteenth-century customers lighted him- or herself to bed. Its wide tray is edged with moulded scrolls and the handle, also in the form of a scroll, has a satyr mask under it. It is decorated in underglaze blue, and enamelled in colours and gilt. There is a broad band of scale-blue with three panels bordered with a gilt rococo pattern and panelled with ropes of flowers. The nozzle is moulded with two leaves painted in natural colours, and between them are panels of blue with gilt foliage sprays. It has the fretted square mark in underglaze blue.

Figures were made at Worcester in the early days, it now seems, but they are very rare and not very remarkable either in quality or originality; so that it hardly seemed worth showing any examples here.

(Left) *'Fable' dish, painted by O'Neale, with fluted sides and osier moulding. 9½ in. long.* (Right) *Spoon tray with a landscape once attributed to 'Mr Fogo'. 6¼ in. long. Dr Wall.* (Sotheby & Co.)

11. The Flights, the Barrs and the Chamberlains

Dr Wall died in the year 1776, but the running of the factory continued in the hands of William Davis, the manager. During this period, therefore, little change occurred in the styles or types of wares made at the factory, and the 'Dr Wall' period is by common consent extended to cover the period up to 1783.

It was in this year, following the death of Davis, that the partners sold out their interest for three thousand pounds to

Plate from a service made for the Duke of Clarence (see p. 47). (Victoria & Albert Museum.)

Thomas Flight, the firm's London agent, who wished to set up in business his two sons Joseph and John. It was not a high price; only seven years before, when one of the partners died, his widow had received £2,000 for a fifth part of the partnership. It may well be that, as the selling agent, Flight was in a position to hold the proprietors to ransom: or perhaps the wares being produced under the old management were proving unsaleable in an age when tastes were changing very rapidly.

Flight was evidently very closely in touch with the needs of the London market—the sons had been apprenticed as jewellers—and after a few years there came about a gradual change in the styles of the Worcester factory. There had, of course, been portents of this in the last years of the Wall period: no factory at that time could altogether have escaped the influence of the strenuous efforts of Josiah Wedgwood and others in developing Neo-classical themes. The sugar basin and cover from the 'Lord Stormont' service (page 50), with its festooned turquoise-blue drapery and gilt fringe, was such a foretaste of the future; Classical urns were also creeping in among the flowers, as in the *déjeuner* set on page 51. From now on—perhaps with the gradual dying-off of the old workmen—the old-style bird and flower painting and the coloured grounds tended to drop away and become replaced by simpler Classical forms and restrained patterns of blue or gilt borders, or small sprigs of flowers. There are also gold-striped grounds and the interesting 'dry-blue' flowers (colour plate and page 44).

John Flight, the elder son, was in charge of affairs from 1783 until his death in 1791, during which time, as we learn from the diary he left, there were many problems in production, heavy losses occurring in the kiln. At one time, it appears, he was even having to import French porcelain to keep up his supplies. For a year or two before his death John Flight seems to have had some technical assistance from a Martin Barr, and in 1792 or 1793 the latter became a partner with Joseph Flight, the younger brother.

In 1786 the firm opened a retail shop in High Street, Worcester, to show off their wares to visiting gentry, and two years later, this venture being successful, they moved to larger premises, where they received a visit from King George III and Queen Charlotte. Their Majesties toured the works, and the Queen bought a service typical of the blue and gold wares; it was derived from a Chinese original, but clearly hits off the new formalized tastes. It is sometimes called the 'Queen's pattern', like that of the Dr Wall days (page 29), but its proper name is the 'Royal Lily'.

The royal visit earned the factory letters patent, and a crown was added to the mark. At the suggestion, apparently, of the King, Flight and Barr (as the firm was now called) opened a shop in Coventry Street, London, and this address often appears on the wares of the time.

The firm made a great many heraldic services for the nobility and the wealthy, lavishly gilded, with gadrooned edges and pearled and beaded borders. In 1792 appeared the large dinner service made for the Duke of Clarence (afterwards King William IV), which bears a painting *en grisaille* by James Pennington of the figure of Hope standing on a seashore in a storm; it has a rich mazarine-blue border, elaborately gilt. Pennington also did portraits of the King and Queen and perhaps the half-length figure of a boy on the beaker (below); the latter is painted in colours in an oval medallion flanked by gilt sprays of barley and hops, with a wild rose in gilt on the back.

Painting from the last phase of the Dr Wall period and the beginning of the Flight and Barr (see pp. 54–5). (Victoria & Albert Museum.)

Plate painted with a shell subject by Thomas Baxter for Chamberlain's. c. 1808–9. (Victoria & Albert Museum.)

These early days of the Flights and the Barrs also saw the use on porcelain of subjects from the sensationally popular paintings of Angelica Kauffmann, published as engravings by Bartolozzi and others. The can (a coffee cup without a footrim) on page 56 shows a figure of Poetry: early as this piece seems to be—Mr Rackham dates it to 1783—it already shows the trend the factory was to take, not only with the figure painting, but also the formal gilt border of the panel and the festoons of gilt foliage hanging from the rim.

Martin Barr, in working out his improvements to the paste, seems also to have been aiming at a more economical production. The new bodies at Worcester still contained soaprock, but they became more opaque, white and hard—a medium admirably suited to the new styles of painting. In the Flight and Barr period the wares were also heavier in substance: some have an incised 'B' which has been held to indicate experimental bodies developed by Martin Barr.

In 1807 the firm was joined by Martin Barr, junior, and changed its name to Barr, Flight, and Barr, although the name Flight and Barr was retained for the London end, apparently the exclusive concern of the Flight family. In this year there was another royal visit from the Prince of Wales (afterwards King George IV), who gave them his royal appointment: the princely feathers appear in the mark at this time. There was another change in the company's name in 1813 with the death of Martin Barr, senior, and the taking into partnership of a younger member of the Barr family; it now became known as Flight, Barr and Barr, a style which was to continue until 1840.

In these early years of the nineteenth century, the firm

Flight and Barr china (see p. 57). (Victoria & Albert Museum.)

continued to turn out its excellent tea services, with much fluting and tasteful decoration. Alongside them it also developed strongly the naturalistic painting favoured at the time, using it on vases and other ornamental wares of all sizes and of Neo-classical or 'Etruscan' forms, as they were called at the time. The names of many of these artists are known, but, as they were not usually allowed to sign their work, only a few can be positively identified.

Outstanding among them, not only for his own work but for his influence on other artists, was Thomas Baxter (1782–1821), whose father had a china-decorating shop off Fleet Street, London; a watercolour by Baxter showing Caughley porcelain being decorated in this establishment is to be seen in the Victoria & Albert Museum. Baxter's first work at Worcester seems to have been for Flight, Barr and Barr from 1814 to 1816, after which he went to Swansea for three years, working for Dillwyn on botanical studies of plants, as well as landscapes and figures. He returned to Worcester in 1819 and worked there as an independent artist until his death two years later.

Baxter, who had studied at the Royal Academy, has a pleasant style and differs from many of his contemporaries in using short brush-strokes or a stippling effect which is perhaps more acceptable to modern tastes than the minutely painted work so much in favour then, and of which manufacturers were so proud. He was a fine figure painter, but

Flight and Barr china. (Victoria & Albert Museum.)

perhaps his best work is to be seen in flowers and shell pieces, like that shown on page 57.

There were several other interesting developments in the period, among them the invention of transfer printing by the bat process, as seen on the coffee cup on page 19. This was an echo of the then very popular stipple engraving as typically shown in the prints of Bartolozzi. In this process the copperplate was oiled rather than inked, and the design was transferred to the piece by means of a 'bat' of glue; powdered colour was then dusted on so as to stick to the oil.

There was also a revival of *chinoiserie* and *japonaiserie*, some of it very pleasant. This was the era of the heavily decorated and gilded Imari-style 'Japans' of Derby and Spode; but the Flight, Barr and Barr versions, to their great advantage, held more closely to the older traditions at Worcester in his field. Two very pleasant designs also appear on page 58. The cup and saucer on the left are done in an attractive latter-day *chinoiserie* in colours and gilding, while the coffee can and saucer on the right has *japonaiserie* of flowering trees and birds in colour and gold.

The chocolate cup and saucer shown above offers *chinoiserie* in a Classical form. The cup is in the shape of a Greek skyphos, with two gilt handles and a row of beads round the neck, and while this is painted with *chinoiserie* the saucer has flowers around the rim painted in thick enamel which stands out slightly in relief on a blue ground.

Looking at the other Flight, Barr and Barr pieces shown in the same place, the piece immediately below the foregoing is an inkstand of about 1830, 5⅞ in. long, with a gilt handle in the form of two intertwined serpents, and two quiver-shaped sockets for tapers at the back. It is painted with a view of Great Malvern Abbey, which is typical of the very large amount of topographical painting turned out by the firm in these years. So too is the pin tray, where the view is of Conway Castle in a storm; the first of these pieces dates from 1830, the second from 1820. The chocolate cup and saucer on the right acknowledges the Classical form, with foliated scrolls and vases painted delicately in colours on horizontal bands on a lemon-yellow ground; this all-too-rare style seems to have derived from Raphael's arabesques and the wall-paintings of Roman villas.

The pastille burner, of about 1815, has apple blossoms in natural colours on a blue ground, with two reserved panels having exotic birds coloured. The plate in the middle of the group is thought to be by a painter named John Barker, another shell painter known only by his name, but whose work is different in style from Baxter's; the sea urchin and shell are in natural colours, and are set off in the vermiculated gold pattern which is another of the attractive developments at this time. Also supposedly the work of Barker is the shell painting on the vases on the extreme right and left of the group on page 58. They are of a squat Classical form, with a flaring mouth, and they are supported on a plinth with three incurved sides by three gilt lion's legs: a very ponderous form for such a tiny piece, but the firm was evidently very proud of it, for it gave them the full names and addresses of the time. One of them has the impressed 'F.B.B.' and crown as well. The vase in the centre is later than any of the other pieces, dating from about 1830, and shows, characteristically of the era, relief work of hops modelled and coloured naturalistically on a pale green ground: vases are found with applied flowers in this style.

Jug painted by Humphrey Chamberlain with a sporting subject (see p. 62). (Victoria & Albert Museum.)

CHAMBERLAIN'S WORCESTER

In the Dr Wall period there had been only one porcelain factory in Worcester. But on the death of William Davis, the old partnership was sold to Thomas Flight, and one of the decorators there, Robert Chamberlain—perhaps the chief one—left to set up in business on his own account.

With him went his son Humphrey and several other workmen, and they decorated wares which had been bought 'in the white', from Caughley and elsewhere. Soon afterwards he began manufacturing porcelain himself, setting up premises on the site where the Royal Worcester factory now stands. The body he used was similar to that of the older concern, but often greyish, with a glaze that was given to crazing. Pattern books issued at this time suggest that he was concentrating on tea services decorated in similarly simple styles to those of the Royal factory, with oval shapes and typical fluting. These wares often bear the marks shown on page 63 perhaps with the addition of the pattern number, which began at successive thousands from one to five. By the early 1800's, however, Chamberlain's seem to have started to make the heavily ornate versions of the old Imari patterns which make so much of their later work so oppressive and dreary. Typical is a large consignment of tea, coffee and other wares ordered by Lord Nelson.

The factory also went in a great deal for the same kind of naturalistic paintings as the Flight and Barr establishment. Humphrey Chamberlain was himself a painter of

61

parts, and he was responsible for some of the better products in this field, notably, it is believed, the jug on page 61.

Although Humphrey Chamberlain was considered at the time to be the equal of Baxter as a painter, his work is almost photographic in the way he took enormous pains to hide his brush-strokes: he boasted that 'a connoisseur could never distinguish the touch of his brush nor discover how the effect was produced'. Many of the artists from the other factory, including Baxter himself, worked also for Chamberlain's but their work is difficult to identify.

By the year 1840, both firms were feeling the strain of competition from the bone china manufacturers of Staffordshire, and the stronger of the two, Chamberlain's, absorbed the older, under the name of Chamberlain and Co. In 1852 this concern was wound up and a new company started by W. H. Kerr and R. W. Binns. Ten years later the assets were taken over by the Worcester Royal Porcelain Company, which operates on the old Chamberlain site today.

If you walk around the fine collection of the Perrins Museum at the Worcester works you may see, arranged in historical progression, most of the types of wares described in these pages; you may also see there the continuation into Victorian days. This is a story of its own, and though well worth the telling, would call for a book of its own.

Four fan-shaped covered dishes and an oval centrepiece from a Chamberlain supper set. (Sotheby & Co.)

12. Marks

(Reproduced by kind permission of the Worcester Royal Porcelain Co. Ltd.)

 1. *The Worcester crescent. Painted in blue or red, printed in blue, enamelled in gold, black or blue. Dr Wall period and (in a smaller form) to 1790.*

 2. *The crescent with additions; said to occur rarely on blue and white wares.*

 3. *Dr Wall period.*

 4. *The fretted square of the Wall period.*

5. *Marks in imitation of Chinese characters. Used on wares in that style from Bristol days down to 1765–70.*

6. *Imitation Meissen crossed swords, c. 1760–70.*

R Hancock fecit
RH. Worcester 7. *Hancock and Holdship 'signatures', c. 1756–74 (see page 54).*

FLIGHTS 8. *Impressed in wares of 1783–91.*

Flight 9. *Flight period, c. 1783–92, in blue.*

63

17. From *1814* to about *1820*.
18. From *1820* to *1840*.
19. From *1840* to *1845*.
20. *1847*, after closing of Coventry Street office.

15 Chamberlain's

16 Chamberlain's
Worcester.
& 63, Piccadilly,
London.

17 Chamberlain's
Regent China
Worcester
& 155
New Bond Street,
London.

18 Chamberlain's
Worcester.
& 155
New Bond Street,
London.
Royal Porcelain Manufacturers.

CHAMBERLAINS
WORCESTER
& 155
New Bond Street
LONDON

19 CHAMBERLAIN & CO.,
WORCESTER
155 NEW BOND STREET
& NO. 1,
COVENTRY ST.
LONDON.

20

Chamberlain & Co. Worcester.

10. *The crown was added to the name in 1789 to mark the grant of a royal patent.*
11. *Said to indicate experimental bodies introduced by Martin Barr when he became a partner.*
12. *The partnership from 1792 to 1807.*
13. *The partnership from 1807 to 1813.*
14. *The partnership from 1813 to 1840.*
15. *Written in colour, with or without 'Worcester', 1780 to 1808.*
16. *About 1814–15.*